# I say...
# BUENAS NOCHES
# TO MY FATHER

By E. Louis Mantsch

A 4am Brain book
4amBrain@gmail.com

This book is dedicated to my nieces, they inspire me with their ability to learn and speak multiple languages.

This book belongs to:

_____

When I wake up…
I say 'good morning' to my mother.

I say 'buenos dias' to my father.

When I finish breakfast...
I say 'thank you' to my mother.
I say 'gracias' to my father.

When I leave for school...
I say 'goodbye' to my mother.

I say 'adios' to my father.

When I come home from school...
I say 'good afternoon' to my mother.

I say 'buenas tardes' to my father.

When I get to the table for dinner…

I say 'hello' to my mother.

I say 'hola' to my father.

When I want to leave the dinner table…

I say 'excuse me' to my mother.

I say 'con permiso' to my father.

When I am thanked…
I say 'you're welcome' to my mother.

When I want to stay outside and play…
I say 'please' to my mother.

I say 'por favor' to my father.

When I apologize...

I say 'I am sorry' to my mother.

I say 'lo siento' to my father.

When I really mean it…

I say 'I love you' to my mother.
I say 'te amo' to my father.